SUSANNA WESLEY
Mother of Methodism

Mary Greetham

If the Methodist Church canonised saints then surely Susanna would have been thus honoured, but since this is not our custom, let us remember her with gratitude, and be mindful of the fact that she gave to the world two sons who changed the face of these islands in the eighteenth century.

2nd revised edition 2003 ISBN 1 85852 251 X

1st edition 1988, Reprinted 1994 ISBN 0 946550 20 4

© 2003 Trustees for Methodist Church Purposes

All rights reserved. No part of this publication may be reproduced, stored in a retrieval system, transmitted, in any form or by any means, electronic, mechanical, photocopying, recording or otherwise, without the prior permission of the publishers Foundery Press, 4 John Wesley Road, Werrington, Peterborough PE4 6ZP

CONTENTS

	Page
Foreword	3
Her Early Life	4
The Little School	8
Old Jeffrey	12
Susanna, the Mother of Methodism	15
Widowhood	18
The Last Years	21
Further Reading	23
Family Tree	24

Acknowledgement

Illustrations by Richard G Douglas.

Richard Douglas is an artist and a Methodist local preacher who lives in Thirsk, Yorkshire. He gave exceptional help to the Greethams during their wardenship of the Old Rectory at Epworth, from 1987 to 1992, and made valuable artefacts for the Old Rectory shop. He also made a copy of the original 'fire' picture which is housed in Brunswick Methodist Church in Newcastle, and this copy hangs in the Old Rectory at Epworth.

FOREWORD

It is a pleasure to commend this short but perceptive sketch of the life and faith of Susanna Wesley. Mary Greetham writes very readably and attractively, and enables us to see what a remarkable person Susanna was – as wife, mother, educator, pastor and theologian.

Mrs Greetham not only brings out Susanna's decisive influence in the Christian nurture of her children, but also her creative role in the development of Methodism itself. Methodists may truly say of her, what St. Paul says of the new Jerusalem, that, 'She is our mother'. This little cameo should help us to honour her as such.

Moreover, in a day when the Christian churches are at last beginning to wake up to the enormous potential of the gifts, leadership and ministry of their women members, Susanna's life and example are an inspiration. May this tribute serve to make her yet more widely known, until her praise is sung not only in Methodism, but in all the churches – and beyond.

THE REVD DR JOHN A. NEWTON

Biographer of Susanna Wesley

HER EARLY LIFE

Susanna was born to Samuel Annesley and his second wife in the year 1669, the last but one child in their large family. Like her sisters she was noted for her beauty. They all received a lively education in the London of the seventeenth century at their home in Spital Yard, Bishopsgate.

The house can still be seen today tucked away in a narrow cul-de-sac, including the attic where Dr Annesley used to read twenty chapters of the Scriptures each day. He had been deprived of his living in the great ejection of 1662 when, for conscience' sake, two thousand priests of the Church of England left their incumbencies on St. Bartholomew's day, 24th August, because they could not agree to the tenets of the Act of Uniformity. The new Book of Common Prayer was the main stumbling block. So they conducted the morning service that day and then left their homes taking their families with them, not knowing where they would rest their heads that night. Such a man was Samuel Annesley. No wonder he and his wife raised such a splendid crop of children. Susanna is the best known of them because she became the mother of two famous sons.

Independent of spirit, by the time she was thirteen she had argued herself away from Dissent back into the fold of the Anglican Church. What her father made of it all we are not told. No doubt he admired the keen thought processes that had enabled her to make this choice. She was, after all, a true daughter of her father.

Susanna met Samuel in London, probably at her own home. She discovered that he too had left the Dissent into which he had been reared, and had returned to the Anglican fold. They must have had much in common intellectually for they found they both came from a similarly strong religious background.

In many ways they were opposites in temperament. Susanna was methodical and disciplined in all she undertook. Samuel was quick-tempered, emotional and affectionate, with a ready repartee in conversation. Was this the attraction that drew them together? Her diminutive figure complemented his own small stature and the beauty of her regular features, dark hair and brown eyes, appealed to his masculinity. They must have fallen deeply in love but they did not marry for some years. On the strength of being offered a curacy at St Botolph, Aldersgate in London, Samuel and Susanna were married on 12th November 1688. He was twenty-seven and she was almost twenty. Just a year later he was off to sea as a ship's chaplain, driven thither, he said, that he might earn more money to 'begin the world with'. Susanna was forced to leave the humble lodgings where they had begun married life and return to her parents' home where Samuel junior was born in February 1690.

On his return from sea there was another short curacy in Surrey, and then Samuel was presented to the living of South Ormsby in Lincolnshire by the patron, the Marquis of Normanby. He must have been proud to show off his young and beautiful wife to the parishioners. However, he was not pleased when the mistress of the local squire began visiting Susanna in the parsonage. Samuel was highly incensed. He could not understand why such a woman should visit his wife and try to befriend her; this behaviour was most unseemly. Samuel told the woman in no uncertain terms to get out of the house.

He was undoubtedly high-handed with his parishioners. Yet he seems to have earned their dislike with the highest motives of doing them good. Eventually the family moved, this time to the living of Epworth where Samuel was installed as rector. The year was 1697. Susanna had already borne seven children, three of whom had died and been buried in the churchyard of South Ormsby.

In those days the Isle of Axholme was still a very watery place although there had been the famous land drainage scheme by the Dutch engineer, Cornelius Vermuyden. Four rivers surrounded the Isle and this geographical fact had made the Islonians a parochial, inward looking, fiercely independent race. They looked with some awe but with more disdain on the little parson who came into their midst, determined to make them good.

Susanna was to bear a child most years, nineteen in all. Her gentle upbringing and cultured mind must have suffered greatly as she worked alongside her husband in his ministry to these rough country people. What made things harder to bear was that, although the living was a good one, being worth two hundred pounds a year, poor Samuel had no head for figures. Thus the burden of trying to make ends meet fell on her shoulders. As the family grew, so the debts multiplied.

On one occasion when Samuel could not immediately discharge a debt of thirty pounds, his creditor had him consigned to prison in Lincoln castle. As usual the family was without money, but Susanna was determined to help him in some way, and she sent him her rings to sell. It says much for her husband that he sent them straight back again. Samuel wrote a begging letter to his old friend Archbishop Sharpe of York and was not disappointed by the response he received. The Archbishop also paid a visit to the rectory, was duly shocked at the poverty of the home, and he left a generous amount of money to help Susanna in her worst extremes.

We cannot help admiring what we know of Samuel, his genuine love for his wife, his indomitable spirit in the face of adversity and his wry sense of humour. When in prison he wrote, 'I'm getting acquainted with my brother jayl-birds as fast as I can; and shall write to London next post, to the Society for Propagating Christian Knowledge, who, I hope, will send me some books to distribute among them.' Perhaps this unconquerable resilience came from Susanna's strength of character which was like a great rock in a weary land to the poor unfortunate rector of Epworth.

Only once did they have a serious quarrel that was of a lasting nature. Samuel noticed that at morning and evening prayers Susanna was not saying 'Amen' to the prayer for the king. This was because she did not think that William was the lawful king of the realm. Looking upon him as a usurper of the English throne, in good conscience she could not say 'Amen' to a prayer of this kind. He wanted to know why. She answered him honestly, and immediately Samuel, who was an ardent supporter of the new order, informed her that he could not share her bed henceforth, promptly mounted his horse and rode off to London.

For the next year Susanna heard nothing of him. Whether the villagers knew the truth of his absence is not recorded, but, as Samuel was a member of Convocation in London for the Lincoln diocese, his occasional long absence may not have been commented on adversely. In any case, at such times, the rector would have engaged the service of a curate while he was away.

It was at one such time, when Samuel was away, that Susanna got herself into hot water. The curate who had been left in charge of the parish was no hand at preaching sermons. The independent minded Islonians took the view that, if his sermons were not worth listening to, then they were not going to church. This worried Susanna, so on Sunday evenings she gathered her family and the servants together in the kitchen for prayers and instruction. First one and then another villager asked if they might join the little meeting. She could not refuse them, and slowly the kitchen became filled with eager listeners until there were two hundred meeting each week. They must have stood shoulder to shoulder, but they did not mind for they were receiving the word of God from one, albeit a woman, who accompanied her Lord every day of her life in prayer and meditation.

The curate's anger knew no bounds. He felt he had been insulted and, to make matters worse, by a woman. In high dudgeon he wrote to Samuel telling him he must forbid this illegal conventicle. Samuel in turn wrote to Susanna instructing her to stop the meetings forthwith. However, she was made of sterner stuff for she believed that she was in the right and she wrote back to him in the following terms: 'If you do, after all, think fit to dissolve this assembly, do not tell me that you desire me to do it, for that will not satisfy my conscience, but send me your positive command, in such full and express terms as may absolve me from all guilt and punishment, for neglecting this opportunity of doing good, when you and I shall appear before the great and awful tribunal of our Lord Jesus Christ.'

Samuel knew that he had met his match and wisely let the matter drop, leaving his wife to carry on her good work. The kitchen meeting served another good purpose. It made Susanna realise that, perhaps, she herself had not done enough for the villagers in the past, that she had stood aloof from them and their problems. Now that she had begun pastoral work among them, she could carry on even after Samuel returned.

THE LITTLE SCHOOL

Although by the year 1711 Samuel was trying his hardest to establish a charity school in Epworth, from the start Susanna made herself responsible for the education of her own family. There never was any question in her mind that she would undertake it when the time came. She chose the age of five years to begin the children's formal education and there was an interesting reason for this.

Her first child, Samuel junior, was very slow at learning to speak. This worried Susanna and, knowing her as we do, we can imagine that she took all the necessary steps to encourage young Sammy to talk. One day the child went missing. A frantic search ensued throughout the rectory but without success. Perhaps she was shouting his name, when a little voice called out, 'Here I am, mother.' He was hiding under a table with the favourite family cat in his arms. This made a deep impression on his overjoyed mother, for they were the first clear words she had heard her son speak, and he was almost five years old.

To Susanna this was a signal to begin his education and she made a resolve that when her children reached the age of five they would enter the schoolroom and be taught by her. In babyhood the children were encouraged to cry softly and to fear the rod, but now the real learning must begin. Six hours a day were to be spent in school, three in the morning and three in the afternoon. The task the children were given on the first day was to learn the alphabet. Of the ten who survived infancy and entered the little academy, all but two of the girls were successful. Such children as the Wesleys must have been a delight to teach for they were all very apt pupils. Hetty, the liveliest and loveliest of the girls, was being taught Greek by her father at the age of eight.

One of Susanna's maxims was 'It is almost incredible what a child may be taught in a quarter of a year, by a vigorous application, if it have but a tolerable capacity and good health.' On one occasion Samuel had watched his wife tell one of the children something over and over again. He remarked to her that her patience seemed endless and that she had told the child twenty times, why did she not give up, at least for the present? But she remonstrated with him saying that, if she had been content with nineteen times, the child would not have learned the fact. By telling him the twentieth time her effort had been crowned with success.

The eating habits of the children were carefully overlooked by the servants and as soon as they could handle knife and fork they graduated from their little table to eat with their parents. They were never allowed to call out for anything but were encouraged to whisper to the maid who attended their needs of the moment. They were never allowed to go into the kitchen to talk to the servants, and drinking and eating between meals was not permitted. After evening prayers and supper the children were put to bed, starting with the youngest.

The children of the rectory were also raised with a very real sense of right and wrong. If they were caught out in a misdemeanour and frankly owned up to it they were not punished, and any good or pleasing thing was praised, for Susanna had learned a sound piece of psychology that is timeless in its application. The belongings of a child, be they ever so small, were sacrosanct to their owners, and a promise must be kept.

When fire destroyed the rectory in 1709 Susanna was devastated. Her own writings, all Samuel's manuscripts, the parish registers and the precious papers her father had bequeathed to her went up in smoke. John, then five and a half years old, very nearly lost his life, but he was miraculously saved from the burning building by two quick-minded villagers who made a human ladder to reach him. This made a lasting impression on his mother for surely he had been saved for some special purpose. There came into her mind a text from the prophet Zechariah, 'Is not this a brand plucked from the fire?' Some time later she made a vow that she would be more particularly careful of the soul of this child, and she decided that on Thursday evenings she would talk and pray with him. All the children were treated alike in this respect and nights were allocated as follows: 'On Monday I talk with Molly; on Tuesday with Hetty; Wednesday with Nancy; Friday with Patty; Saturday with Charles; and with Emily and Sukey together, on Sunday.' Looking back on this period of life at the Rectory, Susanna said in a letter to John, 'Never were children better disposed to piety, or in more subjection to their parents, till that fatal dispersion of them after the fire into several families.'

After the fire it seemed that all Susanna's careful years of training were to be lost at a stroke. Her family of boys and girls was suddenly broken up, all having to find shelter where they could. Some of them went into the homes of parishioners, and two of the elder girls went to live with an uncle in London. The children must have wondered what had hit them after the ordered, disciplined life of the Epworth rectory. They soon lost their refined accents and began to develop the broad dialect of the Islonians. Susanna watched them from afar with a breaking heart. We do not know which families in Epworth received the children, but without doubt people who had not formerly been kindly disposed to the Wesleys now felt they must make some gesture to these homeless 'orphans of the storm'. To add to her troubles Susanna was heavily pregnant with her last child, Kezia, who was born the following month. Who gave her refuge and tended her in her confinement we do not know. One local tradition says that some of the family stayed at the nearby village of Haxey and another says that John stayed in the home of a local minister.

Meanwhile Samuel had decided that the house must be rebuilt, and quickly. The expenditure would cripple him, but a kind benefactor came to his aid, and the burnt-out shell began to rise again in the form of a gracious house that was to cost the large sum of four hundred pounds. It is doubtful if Samuel ever really recovered from this vast expense. Amazingly the house was rebuilt and finished by the end of the year and the family was able to move back into residence. How sad it was for Susanna, for it seemed that her careful training of the children had come to naught. Nevertheless, with typical strength of character, she resolved to work hard to bring the family back to its former ways of solidarity and discipline. That she succeeded is quite evident. Apart from the day-to-day routine that the children had been used to, Susanna introduced regular reading of the psalter and other Bible passages in the morning and evening after family prayers. By this time John was six and Charles nearly two years old.

At five o'clock each day the house took on a more than usually quiet time. The older children would look after the younger ones, instructing them in regular Bible reading, while Susanna retired to her bed-chamber, there to spend a full hour in prayer, reading and writing. This was a habit she kept up till the end of her life. Out of this quiet daily hour came the written meditations which reveal much of her character. One must be quoted:

> *Help me, Lord, to remember that religion is not to be confined to the Church or closet, nor exercised only in prayer and meditation, but that everywhere I am in Thy Presence. So may my every word and action have a moral content.*

In the days when boys were educated if they were fortunate enough, girls had a very raw deal. Susanna had remarked in a letter to Samuel over the 'conventicle' affair that there was not a man among those who gathered on Sunday evenings who could read a sermon without spelling out each word; much less would there have been a woman. She believed that no girl should be put to practical work until she could read well, and she deplored the habit of setting little girls to sewing before they could read. The rectory girls were lucky for they had the benefit of two educated minds as their mentors. When Susanna left off in the schoolroom, Samuel would take over. If the pupils were apt Samuel was their man, and he took especial delight in teaching Hetty, the brightest of the girls.

It was she who helped him with the chief literary interest of his life, his large tome entitled *Dissertations on the Book of Job*. Samuel had written books before and had them published but this one was to be the *pièce de résistance*. His ardent wish was to place the finished volume in the hands of his sovereign, Queen Caroline, to whom the book was dedicated. In the event this was not to be for his death intervened. The task of finishing the book and presenting it to the Queen fell to the lot of John. Yet it was Hetty who helped a good deal in the early stages of the eight-year toil. It was she who would sit at the bottom of the garret stairs with her father's candle, waiting for him to lay down his labours for the day and go to bed. It was during this time that the great affair of the ghost manifested itself.

OLD JEFFREY

The year was 1716 and the month December, the coldest and certainly the darkest part of the year. The servants heard them first, strange knockings and noises for which no rational account could be given. Then the children began to hear the sounds, but all were loth to tell their parents for they feared some disaster might be about to overtake a member of the family. Could it be Susanna's brother who had gone to India some years before? Could it be Sammy who was in London at the time? Or did the noises portend the imminent demise of the rector himself? However, it soon became evident that the noises could not long be kept from either Samuel or Susanna. Indeed, on one occasion, Susanna actually saw the ghost, which appeared to her as a headless badger. It would have been difficult to state exactly what one had seen in the days when lighting was poor and inadequate, especially if it was night-time.

Old Jeffrey, as Emily named the ghost, was at first most active in the evenings although later he made his presence felt at all times of the day. The haunting of the rectory is one of the best authenticated happenings of its kind, because all the members of the family who were at home at the time wrote to Sammy who had expressly written for information. Fortunately some of the letters are still extant and there is much common agreement among them as to the truth of the visitations.

When Samuel and Susanna were told of the unaccountable noises that were disturbing the inhabitants of the rectory, they initially wanted to dismiss them as natural sounds that there might be in any house. However, when they both experienced the strange happenings, they realised that this was an extraordinary phenomenon. Susanna, in her practical way, had thought at first it might be rats, and caused a horn to be blown in every room to frighten the rodents away. After this it appears that Old Jeffrey became busier than ever, although no one except the servants seemed to have been frightened by the hauntings.

On one occasion, in response to the loud noises that Samuel and Susanna heard, they both got up from bed, took a candle and proceeded down the main staircase to investigate. As they descended, the noises accompanied them. Suddenly there was a sound as of a shower of coins falling from Susanna's skirt (when this was conveyed to Sammy through a letter, he replied asking if they had dug under the spot where the noise was heard!). As Samuel and Susanna reached the hall, the dog which had been cowering in the corner came and pushed itself between them, presumably for safety from the unseen visitor which, nevertheless, it obviously sensed.

When Samuel was at last convinced that the disturbances were caused by some supernatural force, he challenged it to meet him in his study, man to man, or, man to devil. Whatever the spirit was, it seemed unable to manifest itself in human form. One of the girls had seen something that resembled an old man in a trailing white nightgown, Robin Brown, the manservant, had seen a white rabbit and Susanna, as we know, a headless badger. These were the nearest descriptions that were given. Sometimes Jeffrey copied the ordinary domestic sounds of everyday life in the rectory. He liked to tease the family with the rector's distinctive knock on the front door, and other favourite occupations were to wind up the jack in the kitchen that was used for roasting meat, to plane wood or to break some of the many bottles which were stowed away under the stairs.

It seemed that the spirit was of a mischievous nature and was intent on upsetting the ordered, smooth running of the household. Without doubt it was a poltergeist, a strange phenomenon which clearly existed and even to the present day there is documentation of the activities of poltergeister. Members of the family were not frightened of him and the fact that the spirit was given a name suggests that they looked upon Old Jeffrey more as an amusing friend than an enemy. Perhaps it was something to liven up the long dark days and nights of that winter.

At the end of January 1717 the noises ceased and were heard no more. There is, however, a tail-piece to this story. In February of 1750 Emily wrote to John at the Foundery in the following terms:

I want most sadly to see you and talk some hours with you, as in time past. Some things are too hard for me; these I want you to solve. One doctrine of yours, and of many more, viz – no happiness can be found in any or all things in this world – that as I have sixteen years of my own experience which lie flatly against it, I want to talk with you about it. Another thing is, that wonderful thing, called by us Jeffrey. You won't laugh at me for being superstitious, if I tell you how certainly that something calls on me against any extraordinary new affliction: but so little is known of the invisible world that I at least am not able to judge whether it be a friendly or an evil spirit.

The letter at least disposes of the theory sometimes put forward that the whole of the Jeffrey episode was a trick performed by the servants or the villagers to upset the Wesley family.

SUSANNA, THE MOTHER OF METHODISM

There is no doubt that John's mother was a formative and continuing strong influence in his life. The fact that he did not marry until after her death says something about this. He saw her as the ideal woman and during her lifetime it would appear that no other woman could displace her. Throughout his life he kept up a correspondence with her and always appealed to her when he had a problem. It was not to his scholarly father he wrote for advice but his down-to-earth, eminently sensible mother.

When the Methodist Revival was under way and John wanted to establish a school for the preachers' children, his thoughts went back to the days in the schoolroom at Epworth. Then he remembered a letter that his mother had written to him in 1732, and the methodical John was able to turn it up and refer to Susanna's educational methods. Perhaps he smiled as he read these words, 'When turned a year old they were taught to fear the rod and cry softly, and that most odious noise of the crying of children was rarely heard in the house: but the family usually lived in as much quietness as if there had not been a child among them.'

Susanna considered that the first task of the parent or educationist was to conquer the child's will and bring him to an obedient temper. She went on to enlarge on this for John's benefit.

> *To inform the understanding is a work of time; and must with children proceed by slow degrees, as they are able to bear it: but the subjecting of the will is a thing which must be done at once, and the sooner the better; for by neglecting timely correction they will contract a stubbornness and obstinacy which are hardly ever after conquered, and never without using such severity as would be painful to me as to the child. In the esteem of the world they pass for kind and indulgent, whom I call cruel parents: who permit their children to get habits which they know must be afterwards broken.*

Susanna summed up by saying that the conquering of the will was the only strong and rational foundation of a religious education, but when this was done the child was capable of being governed by the reason and piety of its parents, till its own understanding should come to maturity.

Some twentieth century educationists have seen Susanna as a harsh disciplinarian, but she must be judged against her own times and her influence on her own children was lasting. She constantly prayed for them and kept up a lively correspondence with them throughout her life. They all held her in the highest esteem and affection and at any time they would seek her guidance with their difficulties.

Susanna has sometimes been described as the 'Mother of Methodism' and, indeed, it was not just her ideas on education that were later taken up into the Methodist Revival. Surely her kitchen meeting was the precursor of the Class meeting. John always took on board what was useful to him and discarded ideas that did not work. When the revival began to gather momentum John was faced with the problem of how to shepherd the great influx of new Christians. He must have called to mind how his mother dealt with the villagers of Epworth when they were temporarily left without a responsible leader. John would have attended those meetings on Sunday evenings, and although he was only seven years old at the time he must have been greatly impressed by the magnificent work his mother had done, and how she had kept the flock together in her husband's absence. Here was an idea to be further exploited. It is always recognised that one of the reasons for the success of the revival was that John knew what to do with the people once they had turned to Christ. What better means than to emulate his mother's action so long ago, to gather the people into classes and to set a leader over them who would look after their spiritual welfare?

It was Susanna who first saw the value of the lay preacher to the revival. John, as a priest of the Church of England, had thought that to preach outside the hallowed walls of a church building was a sin, but he was soon won over to the practice of 'field preaching' by George Whitefield who had started this work in Bristol. He sent for John to 'come and help us'. John quickly realised the value of this type of evangelism and so he 'consented to become more vile', as he put it. From this point field preaching became the mainstay of the revival, allied to John's genius as an organiser.

John had not yet reached the stage when he was prepared to use unordained preachers. Having received the news that one, Thomas Maxfield, had started preaching, he posted back to London, intending to put an end to it all. He met his mother at the Foundery and curtly addressed her, 'Thomas Maxfield has turned preacher, I find.' It was there that Susanna took a stand that was to influence the future course of Methodism.

'John,' she said calmly, 'you know what my sentiments have been. You cannot suspect me of readily favouring anything of this kind. But take care what you do with respect to that young man; for he is as surely called of God to preach as you are. Examine what have been the fruits of his preaching, and hear him yourself.'

Fortunately Susanna had sat under Maxfield's ministry and knew his worth. John took his mother's advice, listened to the young man and, once convinced of a good idea, was quick to take it on board without a look back.

WIDOWHOOD

When Samuel died in 1735 Susanna was to live another seven years as a widow. To her often sad lot as an impecunious wife was now to be added that of a penniless widow. Samuel died in debt. It was one of his dying wishes that he should have died in a state of solvency but this was not to be, and it is said that one of his creditors, a Mrs Knight of Low Mellwood, came to Epworth on the day of his death and seized the whole of his livestock to discharge a debt of fifteen pounds. Susanna did not even have the dignity of being able to dispose of her husband's goods in peace.

Everything in the home that could raise money had to be sold. Even the bedspread that was made and embroidered by Susanna came under the hammer. Years later the woman in Epworth who owned it cut it up into squares and gave them to her friends. As far as is known only one piece survived and it holds honoured place in the rectory to this day. The handsome sideboard that had stood in the entrance hall was bought by the landlord of the Red Lion Inn. John would have seen it in later years when he came back to Epworth to preach and stayed at the inn.

Such members of the family who still lived in Epworth had to speedily quit the rectory. Although Samuel had raised the money himself to build the house, it was built on church land and, on his death, the freehold of the living had to be relinquished. He owned the house while he was rector but not the land on which it stood.

What was Susanna to do? Sammy or John as ordained priests could have followed their father in the living. Indeed this is what Samuel had desired, for then a home would have been secured for Susanna and the unmarried daughters. Neither of the sons had any stomach for it. John was now in Oxford, as Fellow of Lincoln College, and Sammy was safely settled as headmaster of Blundells School at Tiverton in Devon. Let it be said here that all through his working life Sammy supported the family financially, and the members never appealed to him in vain.

Susanna's first move was to Gainsborough, there to stay with her daughter Emily who had established a school in the town. It is probable that she was able to use her considerable expertise in the educational field to assist Emily. In the year of Samuel's death the prospect of Charles joining General Oglethorpe and his second mission to the new colony of Georgia was first mooted. He was taken on as secretary and John was invited to become chaplain to the settlers. At first John was hesitant about going because of his mother's poverty. Ought he not to stay in England and help support her financially? When Susanna was consulted her reply was typical, 'Had I twenty sons, I should rejoice that they were all so employed, though I should never see them more.' Once again she was in the vanguard of progress as she would later be over the question of lay preachers.

From now on the rest of her life was to be spent in the homes of her children. She moved from Gainsborough to Tiverton to live with Samuel, and then she spent time with her daughter Martha who was married to a clergyman, Westley Hall. He held livings in Wiltshire at Wootton Rivers and Fisherton, near Salisbury. Later he was to move to London and Susanna went with them.

The momentous events of the spring of 1738 had not been lost on Susanna. She rejoiced in the new-found faith of John and Charles but was definitely suspicious about the advent of field preaching. It was probably while she was staying in the home of Westley Hall that she received a visit from George Whitefield. She wrote about this visit to her son Samuel, telling him that Whitefield had convinced her that John and Charles were doing so much good that it was undoubtedly the work of God.

From Susanna's prayers and meditations we learn much of what she thought about life. After the flames of the great fire had destroyed all her writings she began afresh to set down her philosophy of life and in January 1710 wrote a treatise on the Apostles' Creed for her daughter Sukey. When John was in Oxford he had asked for her views on the Holy Sacrament and on death. In response to his question about the 'real presence' she had written:

> *Surely that divine presence of our Lord, thus applying the virtue and merits of the great Atonement to each true believer, makes the consecrated bread more than a sign of Christ's body; since by his so doing, we receive not only the sign but with it the thing signified, all the benefits of His incarnation and passion; but still, however His divine institution may seem to others, to me it is full of mystery.*

She was ever a humble seeker after truth and in the letter written to John had also said, 'I never did much good in my life when in the best of health and vigour.' That we know to be patently untrue but it throws an interesting light on her character.

Susanna had obviously talked with John, perhaps during his Thursday sessions with her as a boy, on the ever-present reality of death. In his reply to the letter quoted above John showed the great love and affection he had for his mother and was worried about her continued ill-health. Was she going to die? If so John wanted swiftly to follow her to the grave. He asked her,

> What if you are to leave the world in a little time? Whom God hath joined can Death put asunder? According to your supposition that unbodied spirits still minister to those who were their kindred according to the flesh, not a moment! Certainly not long. Yet a little while, and if you return not to me, you will certainly be overtaken by your dutiful and affectionate Son.

THE LAST YEARS

Once Susanna was convinced that the work her sons were doing in the evangelical revival was the work of God, she heartily supported all their efforts. This was a great turn around for the rector of Epworth's widow but, like John, she was a pragmatist. Once she realised that a thing was good, she was prepared to back it fully. No doubt the idea of instant conversion was foreign to her. She had been a believer from her earliest days, so how could one point to a special moment when enlightenment dawned? John's journal for 3rd September 1739 gives an interesting account of how Susanna experienced what John and Charles had experienced at their conversions in May of 1738. John said:

> *I talked largely with my mother, who told me that, till a short time since, she had scarce heard such a thing mentioned as the having forgiveness of sins now, or God's Spirit bearing witness with our spirit; much less did she imagine that this was the common privilege of all true believers. 'Therefore', said she, 'I never durst ask for it myself'. But two or three weeks ago, while my son Hall was pronouncing those words, in delivering the cup to me, 'the blood of our Lord Jesus Christ, which was given for thee', the words struck through my heart, and I knew God for Christ's sake had forgiven* me *all* my *sins.*

Surely Susanna was granted the experience of her son John at Aldersgate Street, 'I felt I did trust in Christ, Christ alone for salvation and an assurance was given me that He had taken away my sins, even mine, and saved me from the law of sin and death.' Once again we see Susanna as a true Methodist.

She was to live to see the fruits of all her labours. Samuel died with a fervent prophecy on his lips that the Christian faith would revive in England. It fell to his wife to witness the great outpouring of God's Spirit on a land for the most part sunk in slumberous sin. The Revival took off in earnest after May 1738 and Susanna lived until the summer of 1742. The last years of her life must have been happy and contented. After moving round the homes of her other children she was at last able to live with John at the Foundery. Here was sanctuary indeed, now she would be free of debt as she had never been before, and here she could enjoy the company of all her remaining children.

Samuel junior, who had always come to the aid of his poverty-stricken family, was now dead. His sudden death in 1739 was a grevious blow to Susanna, for as her first-born he had held a special place in her affections. Now John would have to take his place as her 'dear son' and it was a task he took on joyously. Susanna complained that his visits home to the Foundery were always too short, nevertheless she did see him often.

Like so many people of her century, she did not suffer from any specific disease as her earthly life drew to a close. She was just worn out. She was seventy-three years old and she had outlived her husband by seven years. In July of 1742 when John arrived back in London after one of his preaching tours he wrote in his journal, 'I found my mother on the borders of eternity.' She lingered in weakness a few days longer and then her spirit found release. She had urged her children to sing a psalm of praise as soon as her end came.

Thus ended a life full of moment, yet lived out in a very circumscribed sphere. Susanna was a woman greater than she knew, for she stamped on Methodism its unique characteristics as an organised and disciplined movement. She can truly be called the 'Mother of Methodism'. 'They cried unto the Lord in their trouble and He brought them out of their distress. He stilled the storm to a whisper. They were glad when it grew calm and he guided them to their desired haven.' Susanna had reached the haven where she had long desired to be.

FURTHER READING AND SOURCES on the life of SUSANNA WESLEY

Brailsford, Mabel R. *Susanna Wesley*, Epworth Press, 1938.

Clarke, Adam. *Memoirs of the Wesley Family*, 1823.

Clarke, Eliza. Eminent Women Series. *Susanna Wesley*, W. H. Allen & Co., 1968.

Harmon, Rebecca Lamar. *Susanna, Mother of the Wesleys*, Hodder & Stoughton, 1968.

Kirk, John. *The Mother of the Wesleys*, Charles H. Kelly, 1864.

McMullan, Michael. *Prayers and Meditations of Susanna Wesley,* Methodist Publishing House, 2000.

Newton, John A. *Susanna Wesley and the Puritan Tradition in Methodism*, Epworth Press, 2002.

Quiller-Couch, Arthur. *Hetty Wesley*, J. M. Dent & Sons, 1903.

Snowden, Rita. *Such A Woman*, Epworth Press, 1963.

Wesley, John. *The Journal*, Epworth Press 1938.

Wesley, John. *The Letters*, Epworth Press 1931.

Wesley, Samuel. A monograph in the series, *Blundell's Worthies*.

Wesley, Susanna. *Prayers*, Edit., W. L. Doughty, Epworth Press, 1956.

Wesley, Susanna. *The Complete Writings of,* Edit., Charles Wallace, Oxford University Press, 1997

FAMILY TREE

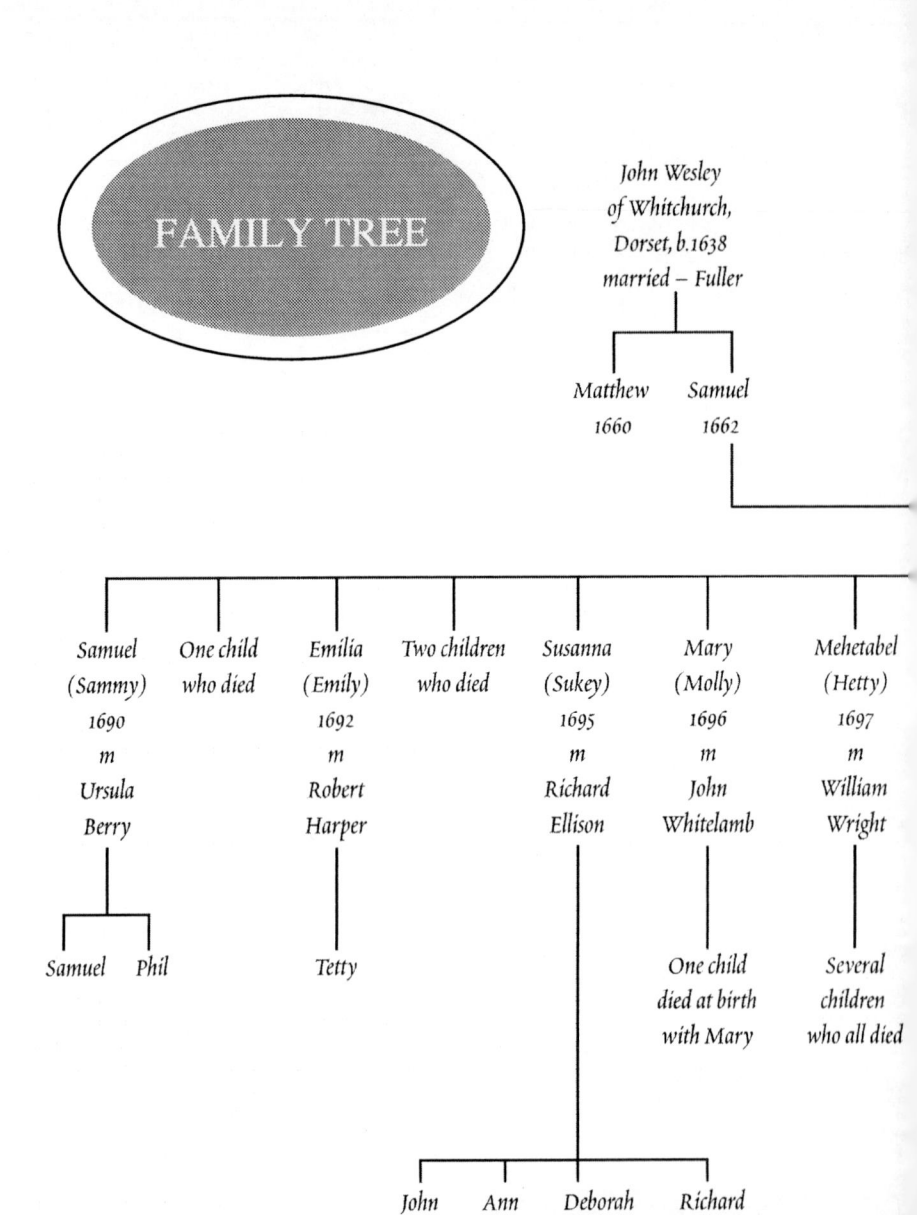

John Wesley of Whitchurch, Dorset, b.1638 married – Fuller

- Matthew 1660
- Samuel 1662

Children of Samuel:

- **Samuel (Sammy)** 1690 m Ursula Berry
  - Samuel
  - Phil
- **One child who died**
- **Emilia (Emily)** 1692 m Robert Harper
  - Tetty
- **Two children who died**
- **Susanna (Sukey)** 1695 m Richard Ellison
  - John
  - Ann
  - Deborah
  - Richard
- **Mary (Molly)** 1696 m John Whitelamb
  - One child died at birth with Mary
- **Mehetabel (Hetty)** 1697 m William Wright
  - Several children who all died

24

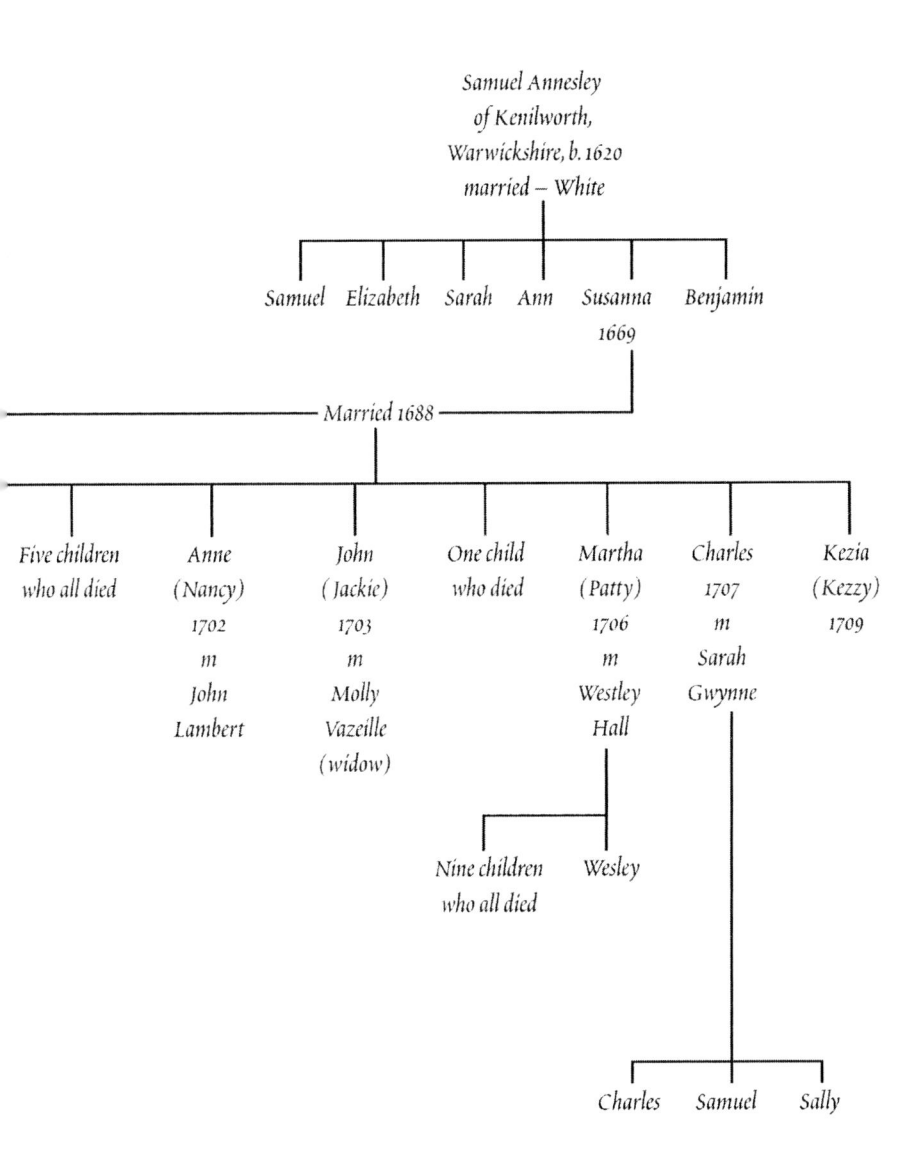

```
                    Samuel Annesley
                    of Kenilworth,
                    Warwickshire, b. 1620
                    married – White
                            |
   ┌────────┬────────┬──────┬──────┬─────────┬──────────┐
 Samuel  Elizabeth  Sarah   Ann  Susanna   Benjamin
                                  1669
                                    |
──────────────── Married 1688 ────────────────
        |
┌──────┬──────┬──────┬──────┬──────┬──────┬──────┐
Five   Anne   John   One    Martha  Charles  Kezia
children (Nancy) (Jackie) child  (Patty)  1707    (Kezzy)
who all  1702   1703   who died 1706    m        1709
died     m      m              m        Sarah
         John   Molly          Westley  Gwynne
         Lambert Vazeille      Hall
                (widow)
```

Nine children who all died — Wesley

Charles   Samuel   Sally

Susanna Wesley is the first title in the mini Wesley Series. Others are:
- 2. Samuel Wesley of Epworth
- 3. Charles Wesley
- 4. The Wesley Sisters
- 5. John Wesley